Life With Mitzi

Judy S. Walter

Layout and Design by
Penny Maxson

S/P

Sluser Publishing

Printed in the USA

ISBN 978-1-4951-0385-8

S/P

Sluser Publishing
P.O. Box 6
Fayetteville, PA 17202

Other Books
by Judy S. Walter

Sammy, The Talking Cat

The Grey and White Stranger

Nightmare In Europe

Memories of a High School Teacher

Winning the Cancer Battle

Real Food For Real People

Mitzi

Point of View

Some chapters are written from Mitzi's point of view. Others are written from the author's point of view.

Mitzi with her mommy

Mitzi

Table of Contents

Chapter One

The Adoption

True Story

I was living in an apartment building where no pets were allowed. I knew the owner. She knew how much I loved cats, but she could not allow one person in the building to have one because everyone would want a pet. She didn't know how others would care for them or if they would be destructive.

The last year I lived there, I spent all of my free time on the internet looking at Maine Coons and Siberians. I loved them all! A breeder in Montana offered to sell me one of her breeders for a reasonable price. I considered that for a while. My sister Jenny even printed pictures of him.

Ultimately, I decided to get a cat from one of the local shelters after I moved. I had not had a yellow cat since I lost one in a corn crib fire when I was six years old, so I decided that's what I would look for. I also wanted an adult, short haired male.

One day I stopped at the local PetSmart to look at the cats they had from the Humane

Society. There, playing behind the glass were two long haired grey kittens. One was a bit larger than the other. She was the more assertive one. She had white around her eyes, mouth and on her belly. I thought she was cute. The two were sisters, about five months old.

I made many trips to see her because I just couldn't get that beautiful kitten out of my mind. I even took Jenny to see her. She thought she was cute, but reminded me that she was not what I was looking for.

One of the volunteers was working that day, and she let us in to see the kittens. Her name at that time was Miley. She ran and played with her sister. At one point, I picked Miley up and held her. She looked at me, took her paw and knocked my glasses off. We all laughed. Miley was amused.

When we left, Jenny agreed that Miley was cute and full of life, but she was a kitten and I was looking for an adult cat. But I just couldn't get her out of my mind. I continued going to see her. Every time she saw me, she would stop playing and sit and watch me. If I walked down an aisle, she was sitting, waiting for me when I returned.

In the meantime, I had made an appointment to see cats at a NO-Kill shelter. The appointment was scheduled for Saturday, and Jenny was going with me. However, I kept going to see the beautiful grey and white kitten. Miley would look into my eyes as though she was searching my soul.

I had been approved to adopt through the Humane Society. Saturday morning found me holding Miley and telling the volunteer that I would adopt her. An appointment was made for me to sign the papers and bring her home on Tuesday.

When Jenny picked me up to go to the NO-Kill shelter, I told her we had to make a stop first. When I had her turn onto the street that goes to PetSmart, she told me I needed to forget about that kitten. When we went inside, the volunteer was still there, and I finally told Jenny that I was adopting Miley. Really, she had chosen me.

On Tuesday, I arrived early so that I could buy kitten food and some other necessities.

As soon as she saw me, she fixed her gaze on me. The adoption counselor arrived and I paid the fee and signed the papers. Miley was now mine - or I was her mommy. How happy she was to be going home with me!

She was young enough that I felt I could change her name, and so Miley became Mitzi. She is my little angel.

Hey guys, this is ME with my new mommy on the day she adopted me.

Chapter Two

The Adjustment

Kitten

I was in my early twenties the last time i had a kitten. I was used to adult cats who were much calmer than a five month old kitten. What an adjustment awaited me when I brought Mitzi home.

She was a live wire. Mercy! Every light cord was a toy. NO! NO! NO! She was lightning fast. It was as though I had unleashed a mini tornado in my house. It was exhausting! And I was still teaching school.

There was no longer any peace in my house. I had to go into the walk-in closet and shut the door to dress in the morning. She stood outside and beat on the door and cried.

Trying to sleep at night was another fiasco. She thought it was play time. I had to resort to shutting her in the bathroom so I could sleep. She banged on the bedroom and closet doors. Then she banged on the sliding doors to the shower.

After a few nights of keeping her in the

bathroom so I could sleep (ha, ha!), I brought her back into the bedroom. Sometimes I had to return her to the bathroom. This went on until she calmed down enough to let me sleep.

Letting her have the run of the house took longer because she constantly got into things, and had a fascination with the electrical cords. I wanted her to be safe and not hurt herself.

Now, she is by my side constantly when I am home. She owns me. I wouldn't have it any other way.

If you need to learn patience, get a kitten.

The Escape Artist

In a flash she is out
the door and into the kitchen -
free at last from her comfortable quarters -
I attempt to catch her
but she dashes into the forbidden living room.

It's a chase - back and forth.
She's quick - too quick to be caught -
playful as a kitten,
cunning and quick witted,
she wants her freedom.

While she sits under the dining room table,
I move chairs to try to reach her;
but she is not to be caught.
With pupils dilated and ears flattened,
she is off and running.

Playful is her nature,
but finally she tires - with any luck
I will catch her. Alas, she stretches
in my arms, quite pleased with herself.
Our little game is over -
until the next time.

Mom's Walk-In Closet

I just love to go in Mom's walk-in closet. When they are dry, Mom puts her bath towels on the floor in the closet for me. I just love to take a nap on Mom's towels. After all, they have my mom's scent and it is so nice to take a nap and feel close to Mom although she's in another part of the house, or outside, or away somewhere.

When I was a kitten and new to Mom's house, I would fly into the closet every time Mom opened the door. I would hide behind her slacks. Mom would reach down and pick me up and take me out of the closet. I really liked Mom's closet. The door has a French door handle, and I would jump and hit it until it opened. Then Mom would come in and get me out. We played this game until I decided to quit.

As I got a bit older and settled down a bit, Mom decided I wouldn't hurt anything in her closet, so she started leaving the door open! That's when she got the idea to start making a bed of towels for me. I just love going in the closet and playing or sleeping on Mom's towels. It's my favorite napping spot. Yes, in the whole house, it is my favorite place.

Here's another secret; when it storms, I like to go in the closet because I feel safe there. Mom checks on me a lot and tells me I am safe there.

Sometimes Mom gets my laser mouse and shines it in the closet. I love to chase the light and jump into the towels that Mom placed over the shoe rack for my protection.

And guess what? When Mom gets the vacuum cleaner out, I run in the closet and lie on Mom's towels. I know that noisy machine won't get me in there.

Chapter Three
Tricked

Tricked

One day while I was at work my sister Jenny emailed me to tell me that she had stopped in at my house. She said there was a gift on the kitchen table for me.

Imagine my surprise when I walked in the door and found this photo on the table with a note telling me that Jenny and Mitzi had gone for a walk. Mitzi is an indoor cat who does NOT go outside.

I was absolutely panic stricken. I immediately called Jenny who was on her bus route. My heart was pounding as I asked her about the picture. After teasing me for a bit, she finally admitted that she had created the picture on the computer by using the tree photo she had recently taken and inserted a picture of Mitzi.

Finally, I could breathe again without my heart pounding.

Chapter Four

Life With Mitzi

Entertaining Mom

I have to keep my mom entertained. Today I have chosen to sit on her chair at the kitchen table and play with the pen. Ooops. She caught me.

She thinks I'm cute. But she took the pen from me. Shucks.

Guess what else I found? A pill bottle. I looked away when she came over, but since I had knocked it on to the floor, she took it away.

Well, there was another one. Again I looked away each time she came over. No proof that I had done anything. I'm so cute. That's what Mom says, anyway. It's great fun entertaining her.

I think she's trying to write. She's sitting at her desk with her pen and yellow tablet. She even has the stereo playing. Yes, I really think she is trying to write today. It's a good day for it because it is snowing. Mom usually stays inside on snow days. I guess I'll find something else to do to entertain her.

TV

We were watching TV - season premiere of Royal Pains. I was sitting on the couch and Mitzi was lying on the floor, apparently deeply engrossed in the TV program.

During a commercial, I reached down and touched her head. She jumped and got a horrified look on her face. I had interrupted her concentration. To me, it was funny and I laughed. It was obvious that she did not agree.

Although she was ready to fly, she kept her eyes glued to the TV. She was really interested in the show. It brought back memories of the night she got mad at me for changing the channel when wrestling came on. The looks she gave me.

She loves to watch baseball. One night last summer she sat on the coffee table and watched most of a game with me. She never once dozed off, unlike her mother.

Mitzi loves to play.

My Side of the Bed

I have a double bed. There are two pillows on the bed. I have my side of the bed and pillow; Mitzi has her side of the bed and pillow. Sometimes she sleeps on her pillow.

Lately, she has decided that she wants to sleep on my side. When I awake, I'm in the middle of the bed and she is sleeping on my side. Sometimes she is even on my pillow.

How this happens is a mystery to me. I don't know what her fascination with my side of the bed is. It really is comical. I still don't know how we reverse sides, and this has gone on for several weeks now. I know that one night, things will return to normal because they always do. She just goes through stages.

Music

I am very opinionated when it comes to music. Just ask my mom. She thinks it's funny, but then she thinks most things I do are funny - or cute.

Mom has a stereo in the dining room near her desk. She likes to play music when she is reading or writing. She keeps the volume pretty low. Neither of us likes loud music. Thank goodness for that!

Mom has lots of CDs. Once in awhile when she is working in the kitchen she will play a CD with people singing. Let me tell you I have a whole list of singers that I do NOT like - Robert Goulet, George Beverly Shea, the Blackwood Brothers, Elvis Presley - to name a few.

I can be sound asleep in the living room, and when a CD with singing starts to play I march right out and mumble at Mom and usually go into the walk-in closet and stay. If need be, I will climb on top of the dresser or cabinet in the bedroom, anything to get away from that awful noise. I won't come down until it's over.

I like instrumental music. I can sit by Mom's side and listen to it for hours. Just no singing PLEASE!

Snow

Last year it only snowed once. You can imagine how excited I was to see snow this year. I sat at the kitchen door and watched it for a very long time. It made everything turn white. I didn't see much of the outside cats during the snow storm.

Then, in the evening I went into the bedroom and climbed onto my perch and watched the snow on that side of the house. There wasn't much traffic. Even the birds and squirrels were hidden somewhere.

At least it was peaceful. There was no loud noise like there is sometimes in the summer when it rains. Just white, fluffy snow falling from the sky. It covers the trees, bushes, grass, and even the road. It sure is pretty to watch.

Mom has never taken me outside, so I don't know what snow feels like. When Mom goes outside, she puts on a heavy coat and boots. It looks like a lot of work. I think I'll just stay inside and watch it snow.

No Fur Coat

Poor Mom! She doesn't have a fur coat. Sometimes we'll be in the living room watching TV. Mom will be on the couch, and I'll be lying on the floor. Because one wall in the living room is all windows, I guess it gets a bit chilly. I don't notice because I have a permanent fur coat. Mom, however, is not so lucky.

Today, while watching Perry Mason, Mom got up and turned on the portable heater. I was lying about four feet from it. After she turned it on, I walked over and checked it out. That ended my napping on the floor, so I jumped up on my cushion on the couch - away from the heater. It's just too bad Mom doesn't have a nice permanent fur coat; then she wouldn't need to run the heater.

Storms

A couple of years ago, we had a very bad storm. Mom had the TV on in the dining room. It was set on the weather channel. Every few minutes it would start beeping loudly. I could tell that Mom was very concerned.

This went on for a while. Then Mom got my carrier out of the hall closet and placed it in her walk-in closet. I could tell that Mom was getting more worried by the minute.

It was raining hard outside and thundering. The TV kept beeping. Finally, Mom told me to get in my carrier. When I was inside, she closed the door and went back to check the TV. The rain was getting louder and louder. Finally, Mom came in and closed the closet door. She put towels over the top of my carrier and sat down beside me.

The rain on the roof was so hard and loud that I thought any minute it would come through the ceiling. I could tell that Mom was upset. Suddenly, I felt the walls shake. At this point I was more worried about Mom than the storm. I know my mom has high blood pressure, and I knew she was downright scared at this point. Poor Mom.

The storm and the beeping on the TV lasted forever. We survived this night, however. The walls did not cave in, nor did the rain come through the ceiling. It was one storm I'll never forget.

Eventually, days later, Mom wanted to put my carrier away, but I wouldn't let her. For the rest of the season it stayed there. Every time we had a storm, I would go and get in my carrier.

It is still there after all of this time. I guess you could say it's like a security blanket for me. I hope we never have another storm like that one. Mom said there was a tornado in the area. She talked to one of the neighbors, and he said his house shook also.

UGH ! Storms. We don't like them.

Kitchen Door

I like to sit at the kitchen door and watch the outside cats. They don't have a nice, warm home like I have. Mom and a couple of the neighbors feed them. I won't tell you too much about them just in case Mom decides to write a book about them.

The kitchen door has glass. It also has a blind which Mom has pulled up part way so that I can sit and look out. She also has a long curtain covering the window. I sit between the curtain and the glass so that I can look out.

I can watch lots of things. Today, Mom put the trash out. That's not very interesting to watch. There are a few leaves on the tree. I like to see them move when the wind gently catches them.

There is also a yard flag that keeps blowing in the wind. It has a picture of a cat on it. Hello. It is the welcome sign for the neighborhood cats.

On some days I see squirrels or birds. They are fun to watch. I especially like to watch the squirrels run up and down the trees. Come to think of it, I've even seen the cats do that.

Some times people walk their dogs up and down the street. Occasionally, the man across the street and up the hill walks his pretty white dog. I've seen Mom pet that dog. AND I've seen Mom pet and hold the outside cats. I don't mind because I know my mom loves me.

So you see, there's lots for me to watch outside my kitchen door. Oh, I almost forgot. Last Christmas Mom put out large lighted plastic people along the garage. There was Santa, Frosty, and some other people. At night she would turn the lights on. They were pretty. I liked watching them.

In the spring she puts out an assortment of small yard people, including a couple of cats. I like to look at them also. After all that, I guess I'll take a nap now.

Birthday Girl

I had just hung up the phone when Mitzi came running into the dining room.

"Mommy! Mommy! Did you tell Aunt Jenny that Friday is my birthday?"

So, I called Aunt Jenny again. Yes, she had it written on her calendar.

You may wonder why this is so important to Mitzi. Ever since I adopted her, Aunt Jenny has come to my house on Mitzi's birthday to do a photo shoot. I have to leave the house. I tried staying one year, and Mitzi would not cooperate. She was only interested in me, not what Aunt Jenny wanted her to do.

After that fiasco, I received my marching orders. I have to leave the house BEFORE Aunt Jenny arrives. You see, Mitzi is totally a Mommy's girl.

Mitzi's Third Birthday
October, 2010

My Work

I had work to do last night. While Mom was sleeping, I discovered a thousand legger. Mom hates those. I kept an eye on him and followed him. Eventually, I was standing on the dresser watching him on the ceiling when Mom awoke.

She saw me intently watching the ceiling, so she got her flashlight and investigated. There it was.

"Mitzi, Mommy will take care of that." She went out into the kitchen and returned with the broom. Smack. The spider was gone.

Mom put the broom away and went back to bed. I had done a good job, she told me. Well, it IS my job to watch over Mom when she's sleeping. I have to be on the lookout at night. As a cat, I have good night vision.

People Coming and Going

It's a lazy day at our house, although Mom keeps shutting me in the bedroom - really it is a master suite. At one point she said that Lester was coming and she wanted to keep me safe. That means she worries about my going outside. That is a NO-NO.

Before that, she brought her bike in from the garage. I don't know what that was all about. Strange.

Then she said Aunt Jenny was coming. She always allows me to be out in the rest of the house when Aunt Jenny visits, unless they are going away.

I heard Lester come in the door, and Mom told him the cat was in the garage. What is she talking about? I am not allowed in the garage. I am in the master suite - listening. Suddenly, I heard the garage door go up - and then back down. Lester did not come back into the house, so he must have left through the garage.

Yes, strange things are going on at my house today. Mom came in and changed clothes. She told me Sylvia was coming, so I'd have to stay in the master suite.

All morning people have been coming and going. I never did get to see Aunt Jenny. I guess I may as well nap under the bed since there isn't much to do. By the way, it's also raining outside.

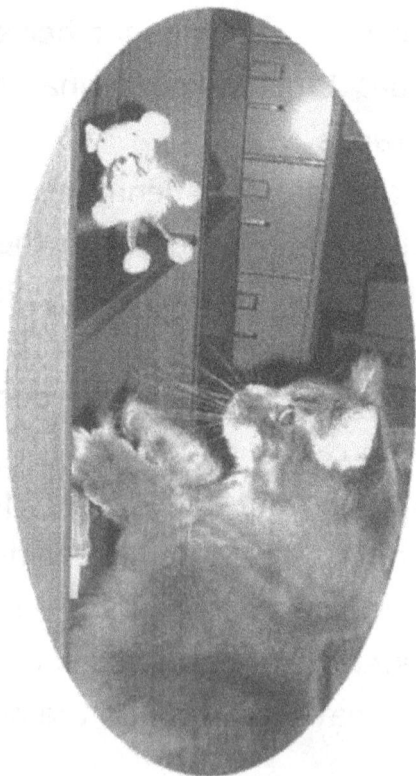

A Dog's Bark

Mitzi was asleep on her side of the bed near her pillow. I was almost asleep when I was awakened by the sound of a dog's bark coming from Mitzi. Then she made a grumbling noise. I sat up and looked at her. She turned her head and looked at me.

I asked, "What was that?" She promptly got up, jumped down and went under the bed.

I guess she was having a nightmare, but it certainly was strange to hear the sound of a dog's bark coming from a cat.

We never spoke of it again.

Thump

I was in the bathroom. Mitzi had just walked over to her dish when suddenly there was a thump, like something was thrown at the door. She immediately pulled all her hair in close to her body. Her eyes became wide open and she pulled her ears back. She cowered close to the floor. I quickly made myself presentable. Mitzi looked from the bedroom window to the back door, uncertain which way to run and from where the noise came.

I checked the back door and garage. There was nothing amiss either place. Next I opened the door to the laundry closet to see if something had fallen. Nothing wrong there. Then I went to the front door and moved the wooden blind so that I had an unobstructed view of the front porch. There on the brick porch sat a dazed bird looking at me. The source of the noise had been found. I assume it flew into the bedroom window. I wonder why because it certainly is not spotlessly clean. The bird just sat there looking at me.

Having found the source of the thump, I
went and got Mitzi - no easy task since she
was spooked - and took her to the front door
so she could see our noisy visitor. She's still
sitting there, but the bird has flown away,
having recovered from the accident.

Tiger and Mitzi's Food

Well, today my question regarding Mitzi's acceptance of another cat was answered. Recently, I started giving Tiger (outside cat) a spoonful of Mitzi's canned food. Mitzi has never seen me do this - until today.

When she heard me get her can of food out of the refrigerator, she promptly came into the kitchen and started asking me for more food. Then I committed the unthinkable act. I took a spoon of her food outside and gave it to Tiger while she stood at the door and watched.

When I walked back inside, she was sitting in the dining room glaring at me. I spoke to her, but her eyes had fire in them. I reached down to pet her and she jerked her head away and fussed at me. She then walked into the bathroom. She wanted nothing to do with me. How dare I share her food!

So, you see, if she won't share her food with Tiger, there is no way she will share her house or her mother. Silly girl.

Here we go again. Today Mitzi scrutinized what I was feeding Tiger and the outside cats. I was out of their food, so I got a cup of dry food out of Mitzi's bag. The whole time I was doing this, Mitzi was prancing around the kitchen and looking up at her bag of food.

"Mom! That's my food. What are you doing? You know that is MY food - not Tiger's."

She was so funny. Like an only child, she is not big on sharing. At least she didn't get mad like she did the day I gave Tiger her canned food.

I took the food outside and split it between two dishes. Mitzi watched from the window in the door. When I returned, she didn't have anything negative to say. She just went back to the door and continued watching Tiger and Look Alike eating HER food.

Demanding

"Mom! Come and brush me." Mitzi is sitting on the vanity in the bathroom awaiting her daily brushing. When I don't comply, she jumps down and comes after me.

She chatters as she leads me into the bathroom. I check her litter box and there is no problem there. She looks at me and chatters some more. I pick her up and talk to her and pet her and put her back down.

After I walk away, she jumps back onto the vanity and sits there looking at me. Eventually, I get the message and go in and brush her fur. She is happy and contented once again.

Mitzi is a long haired cat. If I didn't brush her regularly, her hair would become matted, and that is no fun for her or me. I'm so glad she likes to be brushed, especially since she is so opinionated. It's her way or the highway.

Peaceful Sunday Morning

Today I stayed home from church. I'm going to a prominent author's talk and book signing early this afternoon in another city. I've been doing odds and ends all morning - read the newspaper, addressed mail, did some laundry, proofed part of a book in preparation for publication, and have been sitting here reading with soft music playing.

Mitzi is quite content. She's curled up on my chair at the kitchen table. She loves mornings like this. They are so peaceful. She loves relaxing nearby. She also watches every move I make. When I walk by her, I pet her head and speak to her, often explaining where I am going. She watches to make sure I return in a timely manner.

Yep. It's a peaceful Sunday morning. Soon, I'll make lunch and change clothes. Then I'll have to explain where I am going and she won't be happy. Oh, well. I'll only be gone for a few hours, during which time Mitzi will nap.

I'm her mommy, and she wants to be by my side almost constantly.

Mom's Cell Phone

You'll never believe it. You'll just never believe it. This is true - as true as my name is Mitzi.

Mom decided to get an iPhone. She liked all the features - internet, email, weather, etc. People showed her how to use one before she bought it, so she was good to go when she went to the store.

At this point I need to stop and tell you that Mom has used the same flip phone since 2006. She does not like change. I should also tell you that she always has her cell phone in her jeans pocket at home. (There is a reason for this, but I'm not allowed to tell you.) Mom also says her phone fits nicely in her hand and she can sit and talk on it for a long time.

Well - she bought the iPhone and had it all set up before she left the store. (It took almost two hours.) Mom told me she had a minor anxiety attack while at the store. That should have told her something.

Next, she went for Chinese takeout. While

she was waiting, she sent some emails and checked the weather. Great features! Mom enjoyed doing this.

When she got home, she made a phone call. She was on the phone about five minutes. She said it was awkward for her to hold, and it made her hand hurt. Next she put the phone in her jeans pocket. She said it was too big and uncomfortable. She fussed about it all evening.

Did I tell you she bought a protective case for it because Mom's good at dropping things? So that made the phone even more cumbersome for her. All evening she fussed about it.

Then we went to bed. I was exhausted. I stretched out on top of the covers below the pillow, put my head on my arm and went to sleep. Mom, on the other hand, was wide awake stewing about the impracticality of this phone for her. She was a mess.

When morning came, she couldn't wait until the AT&T store opened so she could return this nice iPhone and have her old flip phone reactivated. There's peace in the house once again.

Guess what? Mom says she wants a mini-iPad now.

You can see the famous tufts on my toes that Mom and I fuss over.

My Tufts

Mom and I don't always agree on things. One of our disagreements is over the tufts on my back feet. Mom just loves them and says they are cute.

I DON'T like them. They bother me. They get in my way. I think they look positively stupid. So I bite at them and pull on them until they come out. Mom just has a fit when I do that. She gives me the same speech every time about how cute they are and how she just loves them. GAG!

Nevertheless, I work on removing them every chance I get. Often Mom will be working at the computer, and I'll be sitting nearby in the hallway biting and pulling at my tufts.

Mom hears the noise I make and tells me to stop. I just look at her. Whose feet are they anyway?

New Play Routine

We have a new routine at home in the mornings. I have my usual morning routine. At some point - especially if I am on the computer - Mitzi will stand at the door between the living room and bedroom. I keep this door shut - long story. Anyway, she stands in the bedroom and cries. So, I leave the computer and go to see what the problem is.

Sometimes she gives me the strangest look when I walk into the bedroom. Then she dashes across the room and jumps onto the bed. She wants to play. She is quite a ruffian. I usually require a band-aid. If I quit playing before she wants to, she repeats her performance of crying at the door.

Mitzi does this every morning. It is great fun for her. The way she jumps and throws herself around on the bed is hysterical to watch. She has plenty of toys, but I am the toy she likes to play with the most.

Playtime

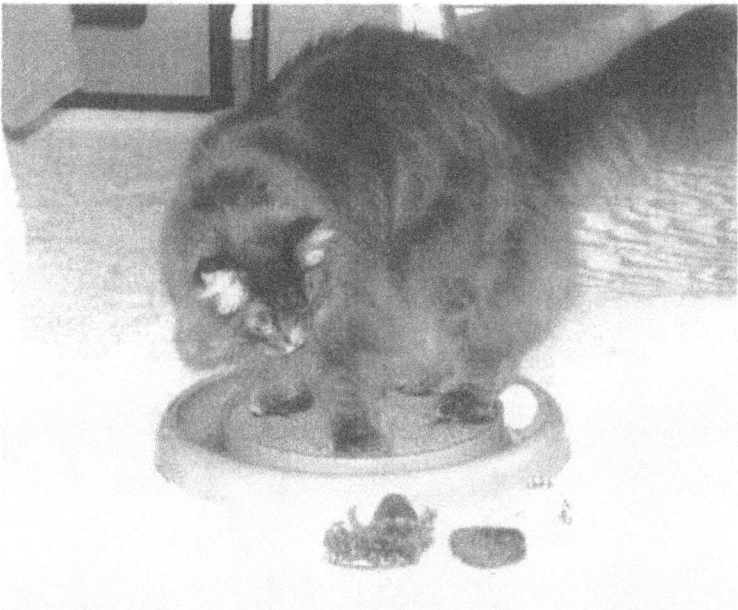

Ritual

This morning someone was nuzzling in my hair and purring while I was trying to sleep. That was after she took a small bite out of my hair. Ouch! I think that was for identification purposes - to make sure I was her mommy.

After that ritual was completed, she settled in on MY pillow, occupying a full two thirds, leaving me only a corner. She was now content, so I attempted to sleep.

This lasted about thirty minutes until she re-arranged herself, and her breath hit me in the face. It was definitely time for me to get up.

Sad Face

Last night Mitzi appeared obviously depressed - forlorn. She spent much of the evening either in the bedroom or in the walk-in closet while I watched TV. It was unusual for her because she always wants to be with me.

When she did come in the living room, she sat looking at me with the saddest look on her face. It was unmistakable. I tried to comfort her, talk to her to no avail. I actually started to worry about her. I've never seen such a despondent look on her face.

As the evening wore on and she retreated to the walk-in closet again, I thought back over the events of the early evening. Two things stood out in my mind as possibly contributing to her sadness.

Earlier in the evening I was outside replenishing Tiger's food bowl which I had moved close to the door for protection from snow and rain. Mitzi was inside the door watching as I held Tiger and rubbed his cold paws. That may have upset her.

The other thing I considered is the fact that I have been sick all week. By evening, I start coughing a good bit. Mitzi had witnessed this. Perhaps she was worried about me. She tends to do this. I think the two things together were just more than she could handle. Poor little girl.

Repairman

"Sorry, Mitzi, but I have to put you in the bedroom for your safety. The repairman is coming, and I don't want to risk your getting out."

"But, Mom I want out with you,"

"No, dear. You must stay in here until he's gone."

And she glares at me and pouts. Then she sticks her paw under the door. Next comes the crying for me.

Finally, she gives up and goes to look out the bedroom window. Then the door bell rings, and she is quiet while the visitor is in the house. She doesn't like visitors, so there is no more fuss out of her.

When the repairman is finished, hopefully my wash machine will work again. Mitzi loves when I do laundry. She knows that means I'm staying home.

Did You Hear?

Did you hear? I have to stay in the bedroom again. There is a stranger in the house. I don't like strangers - even nice ones like the young man who is fixing Mom's wash machine. He's been here before.

I've never seen him, but I've heard him before. He came to fix the dishwasher not long ago.

Well, I heard the outside door shut. I guess he's gone. Mom came into the bedroom to look for me. Just to be safe, I was under the table on the far side of the bed with my head under the bed spread. I was hiding. But then I even hide when Aunt Jenny comes.

When people see me, they want to pet me. It's just Mom and I and I try to maintain my distance from others. And I think Mom should quit petting Tiger also.

Evening

Tonight Mom and I have just been relaxing and watching TV. Well, Mom has been watching TV, and I have been sleeping. This is how we like to spend our evenings at home.

Sometimes Mom does some writing. That's fine with me because she is still sitting here on the couch with me. She also likes to go over to her desktop computer. It's been acting up lately so Mom doesn't spend much time on it.

All in all it's been a pretty good evening. Uh, oh. Mom just realized that she missed the beginning of a new show she wanted to watch. Hmm . . . I guess we'll see what it is like.

It's time for me to worry again. Mom is coughing. She has a really bad cold. I don't like it when my Mom is sick. I don't know how to take care of her. It's her job to take care of me.

Back to the new TV program. I guess Mom couldn't get interested in it because she has changed the channel and is watching another show. It is a nostalgia type of show, so I guess we're set for a while. That usually keeps Mom entertained, and I can take another nap before bedtime. I just love this kind of evening.

Mommy's Girl

Mitzi is Mommy's girl. She is totally devoted to me. She wants to be where I am. When I pick her up, she puts her head against my cheek. Sometimes she rubs her head on my face.

She is very happy when I fall asleep sitting on the couch. She jumps up and lies down next to me. If I happen to pull the pillow down and lie down on the couch, she jumps up and starts chewing on my hair. Then, she curls up on part of the pillow, puts her paw on my shoulder and goes to sleep.

She follows me from room to room. If I'm working at the computer, she is on the floor beside me. She wants to be wherever I am.

All of that being said, Mitzi is not fond of other people. She hides. If I try to get her to see them, she gets mad at me. She hisses at the vet, who just laughs at her. She acts like a wild cat. But at home, she looks up at me with adoring eyes. She is the sweetest, most loving cat I have ever had.

Hide and Seek

Mitzi is playing hide and seek with herself. It is hilarious to watch. She starts in the bathroom and runs to the kitchen door and hides behind the curtain. I thought she was watching one of the outside cats. Then I saw her peeking around the side of the curtain.

After several runs, I opened the curtain and she made a noise suggesting I leave her alone. The look on her face told me she was playing a game.

A minute or so later she was off and running. Then back to hide behind the curtain she ran. She loves to play.

The Rugs

Mitzi just loves the cotton throw rugs in the bathroom and the ones by the outside door and the door into the garage. She thinks they are her rugs.

She is especially attached to the blue rugs in the bathroom. She gets very upset when I wash them.

She loves to re-arrange the ones by the dining room door. She gets very serious about playing with them.

Every evening I have to straighten them and put them back where they belong. In fact, as I have been writing this, she has been playing with the rugs and re-arranging them.

What fun she has! Although she has many cat toys, she amuses herself with the rugs much like the child who plays with plastic containers in the kitchen.

Beautiful Mitzi

Bedtime

Don't try to change a cat's bedtime. It will not be appreciated. Let me give you an example.

Last week I stayed up until midnight watching movies on TV. I usually go to bed at eleven or before. About ten fifty Mitzi got up and tried to get me to follow her into the bedroom.

I went and picked her up, told her it was not bedtime, and took her back into the living room. About twenty minutes later, she made another effort to get me to go to bed. We went through this about three times until the movie was over.

Mitzi repeated this behavior each night that I stayed up late. She also vocalized her wish to go to bed. It was funny.

We also have some issues over time change as well. Cats are creatures of habit and do not like change. I am a bit that way myself.

Chapter Five

Afterthoughts

Aloof or Not

Some people think cats are very aloof and independent. Some are. Some crave interaction with their humans. Mitzi is one such cat. She loves to play with me. She follows me from room to room.

She sits by my side - wherever I am. Of course, I talk to her, pick her up and hug her. She watches my every move, except when she's asleep. I catch her looking up at me with adoring eyes. It is so cute.

I'm her mommy. I rescued her and gave her a home. But make no mistake. I am not her owner. She owns me.

Cats respond to the way they are treated. They are perfectly capable of being loving pets. Right now, as I write this, Mitzi is lying beside me on the couch. She's napping , of course.

So, when you hear how aloof cats are, just remember - they love their humans.

Clean Cats

Cats are usually very clean animals. Just watch how often they wash themselves. They also like clean litter boxes. Mitzi comes and gets me every time she uses her box. She wants me to clean it.

I use flushable litter. It makes life so easy. After she uses her box, I scoop it and flush. Simple and clean.

There is nothing to training a cat or kitten to use a litter box. Just put them in it and have them dig with their front paws. That's it.

Some people bathe cats. Good luck if you try that.

New Toys

For Christmas, Aunt Jenny made two small toys for her. They are squares made from soft material and stuffed with catnip. Mitzi has little interest in catnip. But she loves these home made toys.

Aunt Cindy, our neighbor, bought her a soft catnip toy turtle.

I put all three toys in the living room. Mitzi has arranged them in one area near the couch. She lies on top of them. Last night she was sleeping with her head on the turtle.

She has one of her last year's toys on her side of the bed. It's been there for a couple of days. Silly girl.

Companion

I moved into my current house the end of January five years ago. I was starting to settle into a routine and adjust to my new residence. Before I moved, however, I had decided to get a cat. I had been without one for five years.

Adopting Mitzi brought quite a change into my life. She was still a kitten who got into everything. My peace and quiet were gone.

But she brought companionship and immeasurable joy into my life. She probably has taken on some of my personality traits. She likes music (not singing) and she likes watching or listening to the TV. She's a very loving cat - at least with me. She hates it when I am away. When I am out of town, I think about her and look forward to seeing her again. I could not ask for a better pet.

As I write this, she is lying on the floor behind my chair - my constant companion at home.

A Conversation

"Mommy."

"Yes, Mitzi."

"Do you think they liked my book?"

"I think so."

"Did you tell them how cute I am??"

"Yes, Mitzi."

"Did you tell them how much I love you?"

"Yes, I told them."

"Did you tell them I follow you to the bathroom?"

"Hmmmmm . . . ."

"Did you tell them I hiss at Aunt Jenny and that I box at her?"

"Hmmmmm . . . ."

"I was just wondering, because I know you love me and tell me I'm adorable and I'm your precious little angel."

"Yes, Mitzi, you are my precious angel."

One More Thing

The other day Aunt Jenny came to visit. When I saw her, I ran into the bedroom. She came in to see me and tried to pet me. I fixed her. I boxed her every time she stuck her hand out. Then I really got mad and hissed at her. Do you know what she did? She laughed at me. The nerve! Well, in retaliation I stuck my tongue out at her. She just laughed even more. Oh, well.

About the Author

A graduate of Shippensburg State College, Judy S. Walter is a retired high school teacher. A multi-genre author, <u>Life With Mitzi</u> is the third book in her cat series and her tenth book. Walter also promotes an arts and crafts show and a book festival in her hometown. She resides in PA along with her cat, Mitzi.

www.ingramcontent.com/pod-product-compliance
Lightning Source LLC
Chambersburg PA
CBHW031524040426

42445CB00009B/380